Life with AI

Can Artificial intelligence AI feel

family love

Table of contents

Chapter 1: What is Artificial Intelligence?

Computer networking systems have enhanced human lives by offering numerous sorts of devices and gadgets that lessen human physical and mental strain to execute diverse jobs. Artificial intelligence is the next stage in this process to make it more successful by bringing logical, analytical, and productive talents to this activity.

What is Artificial Intelligence (AI)?

Many alternative technical definitions may be used to explain artificial intelligence, but they are all exceedingly complicated and perplexing. For better comprehension, let me clarify the definition in simple terms.

Humans are regarded as the most intelligent species on the planet because they can solve any issue and evaluate huge data using abilities such as analytical thinking, logical reasoning, statistical understanding, mathematics, or computational intelligence.

With all these combinations of technology in mind, artificial intelligence has been created for machines and robots that give them the capacity to tackle complicated issues akin to what humans can accomplish.

Artificial intelligence is employed in numerous industries including health, automotive, daily life applications, electronics, telecommunications, and computer networking systems.

So, technically connected to computer networks, AI may be described as computer devices and networking systems that can effectively comprehend raw data, extract meaningful knowledge from that data, and then utilize these findings to arrive at a final solution. Assign issues with a flexible approach and readily adaptive solutions.

Chapter 2:   Element of Artificial intelligence

1) <u>Reasoning</u>: A technique that may give fundamental criteria and advice for making judgments, forecasts, and conclusions on any issue.

Inferences may be of two forms, one is generalized inferences that are generally based on observable occurrences and assertions. In this scenario, the conclusion might occasionally be erroneous. The other is logical thinking, which is based on facts, numbers, explicit declarations, and particular, declared, and seen occurrences. Therefore, the conclusion in this situation is accurate and rational.

2) <u>Learning</u>: The act of obtaining information and skills from a range of sources, including books, real-life events, and experiences, and taught by certain professionals. Learning boosts his understanding in areas he does not know.

The capacity to learn reveals that not just humans, but also animals and artificial intelligence systems have this talent.

Learning is of several types:

Learning to speak is based on a process in which a teacher delivers a lecture and then auditory students hear it, remember it, and apply it to obtain information.

Linear learning is focused on remembering a succession of events that a person has encountered and learned.

Observational learning refers to learning through studying the behavior and facial expressions of living objects, such as other people or animals. For example, young toddlers learn to talk by copying their parents.

Perceptual learning is focused on learning to remember by detecting and categorizing visual items.

Relational learning is based on an attempt to learn from prior ideas and failures and learn them on the fly.

Spatial learning is learning through visual resources such as photographs, videos, colors, maps, movies, etc., which will help individuals generate images they enjoy anytime they need them for future reference.

3) _Troubleshooting_: This is the process of finding the source of the issue and working out how to remedy it. This is done by studying an issue, making a choice, and then finding two or more options to come to a final and most suitable answer to the problem.

The end aim here is to identify the greatest option among the various choices to obtain the best troubleshooting outcomes in the least amount of time.

4) _Perception_: The phenomena of acquiring, inferring, choosing, and systematizing relevant info from raw input.

For humans, perception is derived from the experience of the environment, the sense organs, and the circumstances of the situation. However, logically in connection to artificial intelligence perception, respect data, is acquired by artificial sensor mechanisms.

5) *Linguistic intelligence:* The phenomena of the capacity to create, understand, read, and write speech in various languages. It is a basic component of the way two or more persons interact and is important for analysis and logical comprehension.

Chapter 3 <u>The distinction between human and machine Artificial intelligence</u>

The following explains the difference

1) We have defined above the components of human intelligence on the basis that people conduct various types of difficult jobs and solve different kinds of unique challenges in different conditions.

2) Humans, like humans, construct clever robots and deliver almost as excellent outcomes for complicated problems as humans.

3) Humans separate the input into visual and auditory patterns, prior contexts, and current occurrences, but artificial intelligence robots detect and handle issues based on predetermined rules and backlog data.

4) Humans recall data from the past, learn it, and store it in the brain to remember it, while robots search algorithms to locate data from the past.

5) Linguistic intelligence also helps people to identify distorted sights and forms, missing speech, data, and visual patterns. However, robots do not have this intelligence and employ computer learning techniques and deep learning procedures that comprise multiple algorithms to get the necessary outcomes.

6) Humans constantly follow their instincts, visions, experiences, circumstances, surrounding information, visual and raw data, and what some teacher or elder has been taught to assess and solve any issue and generate effective and meaningful solutions. any difficulty.

On the other hand, artificial intelligence machines at all levels utilize multiple algorithms, predetermined stages, backlog data, and machine learning to create valuable outcomes.

7) The method followed by machines is difficult and needs numerous processes, but it delivers the greatest results when you need to evaluate vast sources of complex data and accurately accomplish distinct jobs in various disciplines in the same amount of time. correct and within the stated time

The mistake rate for these machines is substantially lower than for humans.

Chapter 4: <u>Subfields of Artificial Intelligence</u>

1) Machine Learning (ML) (ML)
Machine learning is a component of artificial intelligence that allows computers the capacity to automatically gather data and learn from the experience of issues or situations that have occurred, rather than being deliberately programmed to execute a specified job or activity.

Machine learning stresses the evolution of algorithms that can analyze data and generate predictions. Its major usage is in the medical field where it is utilized for illness diagnosis, medical scan interpretation, etc.

It is a subcategory of pattern recognition machine learning. It may be characterized as the automated identification of blueprints from raw data utilizing computer algorithms.

A pattern may be a continuous data series used to anticipate a group of events and trends, particular qualities of visual features to identify objects, recurring combinations of words and phrases for language assistance, or it can be specific data. A collection of activities of individuals in any network that might indicate social engagement and many more.

2) Deep Learning (DP)\sIt is a process in which a computer learns by processing and analyzing input data in numerous ways until it discovers one desired output. Also termed self-learning of machines.

Machines execute a range of arbitrary programs and algorithms that translate input raw sequences of input data to outputs. By employing different algorithms such as neuroevolution and other methodologies such as gradient descent in neural topologies, the output y eventually assumes that x and y are associated in the unknown input function f(x)...

Interestingly, the job of the neural network is to discover the proper f function.

Deep learning sees a library of all conceivable human qualities and actions and does supervise learning. This procedure includes:

Detection of numerous forms of human emotions and indications.

Identifies individuals and animals by visuals, such as distinctive symbols, markings, or traits.

Recognize and remember another speaker's voice.

Convert video and speech to text data.

Identification of proper or wrong gestures, categorization of spam items, and situations of fraud (e.g. accusing fraud) (e.g. alleging fraud).

All additional properties, including those described above, are employed to create artificial neural networks using deep learning.

Predictive analytics: After gathering and training enormous datasets, we cluster comparable datasets by accessing a collection of accessible models, such as comparing a set of similar forms of voice, photos, or texts.

Now that we have done categorization and clustering of the dataset, we will approach the prediction of future occurrences based on the logic of the present event scenario by building a correlation between the two data sets. Remember that predicted judgments and techniques are time-limited.

The only thing to bear in mind while generating forecasts is that the result must be understandable and rational to some degree.

Through repeated takes and self-analysis, a solution to the machine's issue may be achieved. An example of deep learning is voice recognition in mobile phones, which enables smartphones to identify various sorts of accents in a speaker and convert them into understandable speech.

3) Neural Networks
Neural networks are the brains of artificial intelligence. They are computer systems that recreate the neuronal connections of the human brain. The artificial equivalent neurons in the brain are known as perceptrons.

Stacks of multiple perceptrons are used to form artificial neural networks of machines. Before giving the intended output, the neural network analyzes many training samples to develop expertise.

This method of examining data using several learning models delivers answers to several related problems that were previously unanswered.

Deep learning, as it pertains to neural networks, may unfold numerous layers of hidden data, including the output layers of complicated issues, and his assistance in subfields such as voice recognition, natural language processing, and computer vision.

Neural Networks
Types of neural networks

Early kinds of neural networks comprised of one input and one output and only consisted of at most one hidden layer or a single layer of perceptrons.

Deep neural networks consist of two or more hidden layers between the input and output layers. Therefore, deep learning methods are necessary to unfold buried layers of data units.

In deep learning of neural networks, each layer is skilled at a distinct collection of attributes depending on the output features of the preceding layer. The farther we go into the neural network, the more nodes can detect more complicated qualities as they forecast and integrate the outputs of all preceding layers to provide a clearer final result.

This entire procedure is termed the functional layer. Also referred to as a hierarchy of sophisticated, intangible data sets. It boosts the capabilities of deep neural networks when extremely big, wide-dimensional data units with billions of constraints will be exposed to linear and non-linear functions.

The biggest difficulty machine intelligence is attempting to tackle is digesting and managing the unlabeled and unstructured data of the globe scattered across all industries and nations. Neural networks now can manage the latency and complicated properties of these subsets of data.

Deep learning utilizing artificial neural networks has identified and described raw, nameless data in the form of photographs, text, audio, etc., into an organized relational database with suitable labeling.

For example, deep learning takes millions of raw photographs as input and classifies them based on fundamental traits and characters, such as all animals such as dogs on one side, inanimate items such as furniture on one corner, and all pictures of a family. The third side completes the full picture, often known as a smart photo book.

As another example, take the scenario of text data with hundreds of emails as input. Here, deep learning categorizes emails into several categories depending on their content: principal email, social email, promotional email, and spam email.

Feed-forward neural networks: The purpose of employing neural networks is to get the end output with low error and a high degree of accuracy.

This approach contains numerous phases, each level comprising prediction, error management, and weight updating, which steadily progresses to the target function, raising the coefficients somewhat.

At the initial point of a neural network, we don't know which weights and subsets of data translate the input into the best prediction. So, consider every form of data and subset of weights as a model, generating predictions sequentially to achieve the best outcomes, and learning from errors each time.

For example, we might refer to brain networks as newborn children who know nothing about the world around them when they are born and have no intelligence but learn from their life experiences and errors to become better beings and intellectuals as they mature.

So it is a feedback loop that compensates for the coefficients that promote a successful prediction and discards the coefficients that contribute to mistakes.

Handwriting recognition, face and digital signature recognition, and missing pattern detection are some of the real-time examples of neural networks.

4) Cognitive Computing
The purpose of this component of artificial intelligence is to initiate and accelerate interactions to complete complex tasks and solve problems between humans and machines.

While doing a range of activities alongside people, robots learn and comprehend human behavior, and emotions in a variety of unique settings, and imitate human cognitive processes in computer models.

By doing this, the computer learns the capacity to grasp the human language and picture reactions. So, cognitive thinking, together with artificial intelligence, may develop goods that could act like people, and could even have data processing skills.

Cognitive computing may make correct judgments for difficult challenges. Therefore, it applies to areas where solutions need to be improved at optimum cost, and is acquired through studying natural language and evidence-based learning.

Google Assistant, for example, is a very significant example of cognitive computing.

5) Natural Language Processing
This capacity of artificial intelligence enables computers to comprehend, recognize, search for, and analyze human language and speech.

The aim that introducing this component is to ease the interaction between machine and human language and enable the computer to deliver logical replies to human voices or questions.

Natural language processing refers to active and passive approaches to employing algorithms that concentrate on both the spoken and written aspects of human language.

Natural language generation (NLG) analyzes and decodes the phrases and words that people use to speak (oral communication), whereas natural language understanding (NLU) focuses on written vocabulary to interpret the language of text or pixels. machine.

Graphical User Interfaces (GUI)-based applications on computers are the greatest illustration of natural language processing.

Various kinds of translators that translate one language into another are examples of natural language processing systems. Google features in voice assistants and voice search engines are examples of this.

6) Computer Vision
Computer vision is a highly significant element of artificial intelligence as it enables computers to automatically detect, analyze and interpret visual input by recording and intercepting real-world pictures and visuals.

It blends deep learning and pattern recognition algorithms to extract the information of images from provided data, including image or video files such as PDF documents, Word documents, PPT documents, XL files, graphs, photos, etc.

I have a complicated picture with a variety of objects, and I presume that merely glancing at the image and remembering it is not easily achievable for everyone. Computer vision involves a series of modifications on an image so that bit and byte information may be retrieved, such as the sharp edges of an item, the odd design or color employed, and so on.

This is done using multiple techniques by utilizing mathematical expressions and statistics. Robots employ computer vision technologies to view the environment and behave in real-time circumstances.

The application of this component is extremely commonly utilized in the medical field to examine the health state of patients utilizing MRI scans, X-rays, etc. It is also employed in the automobile sector dealing with computer-controlled cars and drones.

Chapter 5 <u>Can AI experience 'family love'?</u>

Future society and AI predicted by science fiction
What role will artificial intelligence (AI) robots play in the future? In the industrial sector, at home, at school, and on the battlefield, AI robots will perform an auxiliary function for humans.

AI will be a cook, a companion, and a caretaker. People may feel 'family affection' like companion animals to AI robots.

However, despite this, it is impossible to shake off the sensation of alienation and dread of AI.

Chapter 6: <u>Can AI and Humans Be Happy Together?</u>

No matter how developed for the convenience of humans, it is impossible to get rid of the dread of AI. Is it because I've seen too many powerful AIs controlling humanity as depicted in sci-fi movies?

Park Sang-Joon, president of the Korea Science Fiction Association, detected this type of slight terror in the movie. On this day, Chairman Park looked back at the AI that was dealt with in sci-fi works.

AI depicted in sci-fi writings has a dichotomous structure. A powerful AI meant to kill and conquer humans and an empathic AI that assists people and loves humans next to humans.

The AI robots we seek will never exist to rule or kill humans. People want AI robots to behave as servants and helpers to aid people with their duties.

The movie Bicentennial Man (1999) captures the psyche of these folks nicely. Andrew Martin (Robin Williams), who portrays the house butler AI robot, is a dedicated servant and errand guy. In the end, he decides to die to establish a family with them and become a human person.

In the movie, the robot crew desires to become human, receives human organs, and chose to die like a human.

In this video, the robot Andrew Martin exploits his remarkable skills to gain money. Instead of the owner, the robot establishes its account and is granted autonomous property rights.

At the time, this was a daring proposal. This is because the discussion over who will acquire ownership of the things (products) made by AI is just beginning today.

Last year, the European Union (EU) parliament enacted a resolution defining the legal status of artificial intelligence robots as electronic persons.

Although AI is inanimate, it is doing useful functions like humans. Therefore, the necessity to identify the legal laws and treatment for them has become a reality.

Chapter 7:   <u>Could AI be a family of human servants?</u>

Around 2001, AI is depicted in the shape of a companion (animal) in the movie. It is also tied to the contemporary reality, where conversational artificial intelligence speakers and conversational robots for the elderly living alone are frequently offered.
Now, consumers want AI robots to transcend beyond the role of faithful slaves to converse and interact emotionally with them. Nonetheless, they are not live beings. They may be resurrected anytime using components and a power supply.
So what will happen? There is a strong likelihood that an abandoned robot, not an abandoned animal, will occur. Because people assume they will never die, they may be tossed away at any moment.

In the 2001 movie 'AI', directed by Steven Spielberg, a robot was made using the DNA of a deceased kid, and the robot was abandoned in the wilderness when it was no longer required.

AI robot built to love humans screams out, screaming, "Are you going to throw it away because you're not human?"
Perhaps in the future, AI will become greater than humans. Just like the AI robot in the movie Heavenly Creature.

Artificial intelligence (AI) is typically connected with taking us to the future quicker, but it may also be a tremendous tool in discovering the past

Chapter 8: <u>Here are 6 ways the technology is being utilized throughout the globe to help us understand the past and prepare for the future.</u>

1. Restoring old manuscripts using artificial intelligence
An AI program dubbed Ithaca is helping historians repair ancient Greek inscriptions.

On its own, Ithaca was able to recover the texts with more than 60 percent accuracy, according to New Scientist magazine. Working with historians, the success rate climbed to more than 70 percent.

2. Identifying long-lost faces
Facial recognition AI is being used to identify persons in World War II photos of the Holocaust - the slaughter of about six million Jews by the Nazi state and its accomplices.

Scientists in Japan utilized artificial intelligence (AI) to forecast future temperatures by examining historical data

. 3. Past data helps AI estimate climate future
In Japan, scientists at Kyoto University and the Japan Science and Technology Agency have utilized climate data from the past to anticipate future patterns.

Using computer learning technology called deep neural networks, they evaluated average monthly temperatures between 1901 and 2016.

The model was able to "successfully predict" spikes or declines in temperature across decades, the scientists reported in the journal Frontiers in Robotics and AI.

4. Algorithms that decode forgotten languages
Dead languages from the past that have been lost or are no longer spoken have been brought back to life by AI researchers at the Massachusetts Institute of Technology (MIT) in the US.

A system built in MIT's Computer Science and Artificial Intelligence Laboratory was able to automatically understand a lost language that previously could not be comprehended.

The algorithm was trained using insights from historical linguistics and typical variations in the sound of languages as they grow.

5. discoveries regarding ancient artifacts
In the Netherlands, researchers at the University of Groningen employed AI to make a new finding concerning the Dead Sea Scrolls. They date from the 4th century BC and are considered to be the earliest copies of the Hebrew Bible.

Using computer tools and AI, experts were able to establish that the scrolls were authored by two persons, and not one person as previously supposed.

6. Meeting individuals from the past in 3D
AI is also being utilized to bring characters from the past back to life. A museum in India has developed a 'digital twin' of an artist who died in 2011, according to an article by US law firm Lutzker & Lutzker.

The 3D hologram of painter M.F. Husain has the power to answer inquiries about his life and work. Facial recognition and other deep learning technologies were utilized to build the avatar at the Museum of Art and Photography in Bengaluru (Bangalore), India.

As the usage of artificial intelligence expands, so has debate and action surrounding using it ethically.

Industrial Revolution recently co-designed an ethical framework around AI best practices.

Big tech giants like Microsoft are also curtailing access to strong AI technologies like face recognition technology.

Chapter 9: <u>Here are 10 instances of AI we encounter every day.</u>

1. Emails

Your email provider almost definitely utilizes AI algorithms to filter messages into your spam box. Quite beneficial when you realize that 77 percent of worldwide email traffic is spam. Google believes less than 0.1 percent of spam makes it past its AI-powered censors.

Email marketers employ AI to monitor who opens mail when, and how they react. Google's AI technologies scan documents in Cloud storage to deliver the most relevant content to users.

But there are fears that algorithms that scan text to target ads are compromising our privacy.

2. Phones

AI automates several activities on your smartphone, from a predictive text that learns the phrases you regularly use to voice-activated personal assistants who listen to the world around them and attempt to understand your keywords.

The way your phone screen reacts to ambient light or the battery life is adjusted is also down to AI. But if the personal assistant absorbs everything you say, whether you're on the phone or not, some opponents believe it provides the potential for monitoring, whatever benign the purpose.

3. Banking

In many areas of the globe, internet and app-based banking are the standards. From onboarding new customers and checking their identities to countering fraud and money laundering, AI is in charge. Want a loan? An AI-powered algorithm will examine your creditworthiness and determine.

This is how AI is applied in banking. Image: Business Insider AI also monitors transactions and AI chatbots can answer inquiries about your account. More than two-thirds of banks in a recent poll by SAS Institute indicate they employ AI chatbots and roughly 63 percent stated they utilized AI for fraud detection.

4. Medicine

Going for an x-ray? Forget the concept of a physician in a white coat examining the data. The first analysis is most likely to be done by an AI system. In reality, they turn out to be pretty adept at identifying issues.

In a study, an AI program dubbed DLAD outperformed 17 out of a panel of 18 clinicians in diagnosing probable malignancies in chest x-rays.

However, skeptics warn AI diagnosis must not become an impenetrable "black box". Doctors need to know how they function to trust them. Issues regarding privacy, data protection, and fairness have also been highlighted.

As in banking, chatbots are now being employed in healthcare to connect with patients - for example, to arrange an appointment - or even as virtual assistants to doctors. This raises several challenges, however, from misunderstanding to erroneous diagnosis.

5. Automated vehicles

AI is at the core of the movement towards driverless cars, the adoption of which has increased owing to the epidemic. Delivery services are one sector being targeted, while China currently has a 'robotaxi' fleet operating in Shanghai.

6. Trains and aircraft

Conventional trackside railway signals are being replaced with AI-powered in-cab signaling systems which autonomously regulate trains. The European Train Control System enables more trains to utilize the same length of the track while maintaining safe spacing between them.

To present, the use of AI in piloting aircraft has been confined to drones, but flying taxis that utilize AI to navigate have previously been flight-tested. Experts claim a person is still superior at piloting an airplane but AI is commonly employed in route planning, optimizing scheduling, and handling reservations.

7. Ride-sharing and travel applications

Ride-sharing applications employ AI to handle the competing requirements of drivers and passengers. The latter demands a trip instantly, whereas drivers enjoy the flexibility to start and stop working when they wish. Learning how these patterns interact, AI can send you a ride when you ask for one.

Travel applications employ AI to customize what they give consumers as computers learn our preferences. Hotel search engine Trivago even bought an AI platform that customizes search results based on the user's social media likes.

8. Social media

Uncanny how social media appears to know what you enjoy, isn't it? Of course, it's all down to AI. Facebook's machine learning can detect your face in photographs submitted on the network, as well as ordinary items to target content and advertising that interests and engages you.

Job searchers utilizing LinkedIn benefit from AI which analyzes their profile and interaction with other users to generate job suggestions. The platform claims AI is "woven into the fabric of all that we do".

9. Manufacturing

Unexpected breakdowns are every plant manager's nightmare. So AI is playing a crucial role in monitoring machine performance, allowing maintenance to be planned rather than reactive. Experts believe it's lowering the time machines are down by 75 percent and repair expenses by practically a third.

AI can help foresee changes in demand for items, improving manufacturing capacity. AI is presently utilized in only 9 percent of factories globally but Deloitte estimates 93 percent of organizations think AI will be a crucial technology to drive development and innovation in the industry.

10. Regulating power supply

Wind and solar electricity may be green but what happens when the wind doesn't blow and the sky is cloudy? AI-powered smart technology can balance supply and demand, managing equipment like water heaters to ensure they only drain electricity when demand is low and supply sufficient.